Lo

Maquina

"AUSTRALIA 96-97"

IMAGES OF AUSTRALIA
THE RED CENTRE

Photography
PETER LIK

Tanglewood Press

Front cover: Uluru
Back cover: Simpson Desert
Title page: Rainbow Valley

ISBN 0 947 163 22 0

© Tanglewood Press, 1995

Published by Tanglewood Press, an imprint of
GAP Publishing, 44 Wendell St, Norman Park,
Queensland 4170, Australia.

Printed in Hong Kong

Introduction

The Red Centre, an area covering approximately 300,000 square kilometres, contains some of the most spectacular landforms in Australia and has the rare distinction of two World Heritage listings. The colours of the landscape are intensified by the clear outback sky and intense desert sun, creating brilliant oranges, reds, purples and blue-greys.

Aborigines believe the landscape was formed in the Dreamtime (creation time) by ancestral beings who travelled the land and left traces of their travels in the form of land features such as Uluru, Devil's Marbles and Kata Tjuta. The colourful stories of their travels have been passed on from generation to generation - stories now shared with visitors to the area.

Geologists believe some of the landforms were created nearly 2000 million years ago. They believe Uluru had its origins 600 million years ago when the area was covered by an inland sea, and erosion by wind and rain has created the existing rock formation. Uluru is undoubtedly the best-known feature of the area - it rises 348 metres above the surrounding plain with a circumference of almost 9 kilometres.

Whatever your beliefs about the origins of the Red Centre, it has a special magic that can be seen on foot, from the back of a Harley Davidson motorcycle or the comfort of an air-conditioned vehicle. The visitor can experience the harshness of the desert or the tranquility of a lushly vegetated waterhole, staying in accommodation ranging from 5-star luxury to camping under the stars.

For further information:
Central Australian Tourism Industry Association Inc.
P.O.Box 2227
Alice Springs
Northern Territory 0871
Phone: (089) 52 5800
Fax: (089) 53 0295

Ayers Rock Resort

Cabbage Palms - Palm Valley

Cave - Palm Valley

Alice Springs, with East and West
MacDonnell Ranges in the background

Overleaf: Heavitree Range, part of the West MacDonnell Ranges

Camel

Dingo

Simpson Desert

Rainbow Valley

Overleaf: Uluru

Parakeelya flowers

Desert flowers,
Uluru - Kata Tjuta National Park

Xanthorrhoea - Gosse Bluff

Malaku Wiltja (Shelter Cave) - Uluru

Sturt's desert rose

West MacDonnell Ranges

Overleaf: Trephina Gorge, East MacDonnell Ranges

Palm Valley

Uluru

Uluru

Ayers Rock Resort, with Uluru in the background

Kata Tjuta

Finke Gorge

Overleaf: Dalhousie - ruins

Ancient rock art - Uluru

Kings Canyon

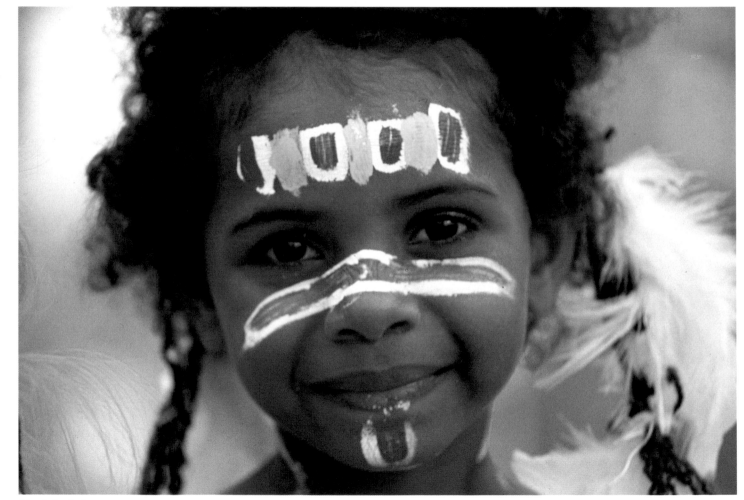

Aboriginal dancer

Ewaninga rock carvings

Chambers Pillar

Overleaf: Kata Tjuta

Sturt's desert pea

Simpson Desert

Uluru

Uluru

Glen Helen Gorge, West MacDonnell Ranges

Ghost gum, Kings Canyon

Kings Canyon

Hairy Mulla Mulla

East MacDonnell Ranges, looking towards
Harts Range

Overleaf: Devils Marbles

Thorny Devil

Simpson Desert

Standley Chasm

Standley Chasm

Ormiston Gorge

Kings Canyon

Peter Lik International Photography/Hot Stock Image Library
P.O.Box 2529 Cairns Qld. 4870 Australia

Phone: (070) 313790
Fax: (070) 313750

Peter Lik's obsession with photography has taken him on many journeys exploring Queensland and beyond. Using his Fuji 617 panoramic camera, Peter captures the beauty and diversity of Australia's spectacular landscape - from reef to rainforest and from the coast to the outback.

The panoramic technique has become Peter's trademark. As a contract photographer for the Queensland Tourist and Travel Corporation, Peter's images appear in many publications promoting Queensland worldwide.

Peter Lik's unique photographs of Queensland are to be published in a series of books entitled 'Images of Queensland' and 'Images of Australia'.